Petrushka

STORIES OF THE BALLETS
Petrushka

Geoffrey Ashton

BARRON'S

Woodbury, N.Y. • London • Toronto • Sydney

Also in this series:
SWAN LAKE
THE NUTCRACKER
GISELLE

First published in Great Britain 1985
by Aurum Press Ltd.

First U.S. Edition 1985 by Barron's Educational Series,
Inc.

Copyright © text Geoffrey Ashton 1985

This book has been
produced by Aurum Press
Ltd., 33 Museum Street,
London WC1A 1LD.

Edited and illustrated by
E.T. Archive Ltd, 15 Lots Road, London SW10 0QH.

Designed by Julian Holland

All inquiries should be addressed to:
Barron's Educational Series, Inc.
113 Crossways Park Drive
Woodbury, New York 11797

Library of Congress Catalog Card No. 85-13562
International Standard Book No. 0-8120-5671-X

Printed in Belgium
567   9 8 7 6 5 4 3 2 1

Front cover: Mikhail Baryshnikov in the television production
The Magic of Dance (Zoe Dominic)
Back cover: Design for *Petrushka* by Alexandre Benois (E T Archive)
Endpapers: Design for Act I of the 1911 production by
Alexandre Benois (Marina Henderson)
Title-page: Peasant Dance, Act I. Royal Ballet, 1957 (Mike Davis)

Contents

Geoffrey Ashton has organized a number of exhibitions on
art and theater, the most recent being a celebration of
the 250th anniversary of the Royal Opera House, Covent
Garden. A tutor to Sotheby's Works of Art Course in London,
he is currently preparing a catalog of the Garrick Club's
unique collection of theatrical paintings.

The Plot

Scene 1

Admiralty Square, St Petersburg in 1830 during the three days of revels before Lent of Haslenitsa or Butter Week. A fair is in progress. To the left is a booth with two gypsy fortune tellers and an old man with an immensely long beard. To the right are stalls selling sweets and toys; in the centre a booth screened from the public by a curtain.

The stage is filled with a swirling crowd bent on pleasure. A group of peasants stamp and dance to a concertina, and others dance to a hurdy-gurdy. Quite suddenly, two

drummer boys appear from the booth in the centre and beat violently on their drums. Somebody blows a whistle and the old Showman appears through the curtains. He pulls back the curtains to reveal three compartments, each containing a sprawled-out puppet—in the centre, a Ballerina, to the left, a fierce black man, the Moor, and to the right, a sad clown, Petrushka. The Showman gives a signal and the puppets begin to dance, coming out of the booth amongst the crowd. The crowd applauds but suddenly the puppets collapse to the ground and the scene is over.

The Butter Week Fair in Admiralty Square, St Petersburg painted in 1948 from an earlier design by Alexandre Benois

Scene 2

Petrushka's room—small, dark, a low door to the left.

Petrushka is kicked through the door into his room by the Showman. He is sad and angry and tries to escape, but without success. The door that he cannot find suddenly opens to let in the Ballerina. Petrushka is intoxicated with her beautiful red cheeks and pointy toes and tries to impress her with a series of magnificent leaps. She is a difficult lady to please, however, and soon leaves without a word of praise. Petrushka is heartbroken and keeps running at the wall until he breaks through one of the panels and hangs, half in and half out of the room.

Scene 3

The Moor's room—large and luxurious with a decoration of palm trees. In the centre there is a daybed.

The Moor lies on the daybed, first playing with and then trying to break a coconut with his scimitar. He fails and suspects magic is at work as the Ballerina enters carrying a toy trumpet. She dances and the Moor watches with fascination, forgetting all about his coconut. He finally pulls her onto his knee and is about to show his appreciation when Petrushka appears. The Moor feels guilty and furious and kicks Petrushka out of the room.

Scene 4

As Scene 1 but later in the day. Night is an hour or so away.

The crowds are thinking of going home but a number of energetic coachmen try to cajole some nursemaids into a dance. They do not entirely succeed and the nursemaids dance amongst themselves. Others arrive, including a merchant with pretty girls on each arm, a performing bear, a ribbon- and lace-seller and finally, a merry party with their faces covered with masks. The light fades and a dreadful noise is heard from the booth in the centre. The curtain shakes and out jumps Petrushka followed by the Moor slashing with his scimitar. He is followed by the Ballerina but she is too late to save Petrushka, if, indeed, she wanted to. Petrushka is killed by the swirling scimitar and falls dead into the snow as the Moor and Ballerina run away. A shocked crowd gathers and a policeman is sent to fetch the Showman. He calms everyone by shaking out some of Petrushka's sawdust and drags the puppet back into the booth as the crowd departs. All at once there is a terrible, unearthly shriek and over the top of the booth appears the tortured ghost of Petrushka. The Showman drops the puppet and runs quickly into the night.

The Showman sees the ghost of Petrushka above the booth, drawn for Boris Kochno in 1950 by Alexandre Benois

The Ballets Russes

Petrushka was first produced in the Théâtre de Châtelet, Paris on 13 June 1911. It was one of the most important moments in the history of dance. Three men, Igor Stravinsky, Alexandre Benois and Mikhail Fokine, had combined their considerable stores of genius to create a ballet, in which music, choreography and design all complemented each other to perfection.

The production was one of the greatest achievements of Diaghilev's Ballets Russes seasons in Paris, the watershed of twentieth-century ballet theatre. It was Diaghilev who brought the three together; Benois was an old friend who introduced Fokine, although Diaghilev must have been aware of him at the Imperial Ballet in St Petersburg, and Stravinsky was a Diaghilev discovery who had stepped in at the last moment to provide the score for The Firebird, one of the successes of the 1910 season. Unfortunately, although Diaghilev had a great gift for bringing together the right creative artists at just the right moment he had no talent at all for keeping them together. After Petrushka he had one of the most violent of many quarrels with Benois and the two close friends were estranged for a time. Fokine managed to stay on another year but then felt that he had to leave mainly because of Diaghilev's policy of promoting Nijinsky as the main choreographer of the company. He returned to choreograph two productions in 1914 but found Diaghilev impossibly overbearing. Stravinsky was an indispensable asset to the company and altogether too useful for Diaghilev to allow anything to come between them.

Despite his evidently highly strung and sometimes self-indulgent nature, Diaghilev was an impresario of genius. The Ballets Russes seasons in Paris before the First World War are the best known and most celebrated in the history of ballet. It was to Diaghilev, the master impresario and publicist, that the seasons owed not only their very existence but also their contemporary notoriety and subsequent fame.

Serge Diaghilev was the son of a nobleman and spent his childhood and youth in Perm in the Urals. His father had made and lost a fortune in manufacturing and Diaghilev grew up in an atmosphere of genteel financial restraint. After finishing his schooling at home he moved to St Petersburg in 1890 to study law. He also found time to take lessons in singing and musical composition from a number of teachers including Rimsky-Korsakov. He developed a broader interest in the arts, however, and a large portion of an inheritance left to him by his mother was spent on financing several tours of art galleries in Western Europe. In

Portrait of Serge Diaghilev (1872–1929) over a proscenium arch from which the Showman from Petrushka *draws the curtains to reveal a scene from* Le Pavillon d'Armide; Petrushka *hides in a corner. Painted in 1954 by Alexandre Benois*

St Petersburg his cousin, Dima Filosofov, introduced him into a circle of articulate and artistic young men who called themselves 'The Pickwickians'. The group included a number of members who were later to play important roles in the formation of the Ballet Russes, including Constantine Somov, Leon Bakst and, the 'president' of the club, Alexandre Benois. Diaghilev was regarded initially as a provincial ignoramus but, apart from having more energy than anyone else in the group, he was socially acquisitive, curious and intelligent and quickly discovered a talent for organizing all those around him.

The first result of Diaghilev's practical genius was the publication in 1899 of the magazine, *Mir Iskusstva* (*The World of Art*). The magazine lasted for six years and was not only lavishly and beautifully produced but also published examples of the work of many young contemporary Russian artists. It had a profound impact on Russian taste and culture in the early twentieth century and gave Diaghilev the confidence to plan bigger and better artistic triumphs. He held only a junior position at the Imperial Ballet but, encouraged by other members of the group, decided that Delibes' ballet *Sylvia* was unaccountably missing from the repertoire of the company and should be produced immediately. Plans were well advanced before Diaghilev received the news that he had been dismissed because he had overstepped his authority. Never again would he be able to hold an official position.

Diaghilev's next major project was the huge exhibition of Russian portraits held at the Torrida Palace in 1905. The following year he took a modified version of the exhibition to Paris and began to realize that there was a vast untapped potential audience for the export of Russian culture. In 1907 he organized a series of Russian concerts at the Paris Opéra and the French public was treated to performances from Chaliapine and Rachmaninov, and the conducting of Nikish. In 1908 it was the turn of the Russian opera and eight performances of *Boris Godunov* by Mussorgsky were given with Chaliapine singing Boris. Initially, the purely musical side of the short Paris seasons was Diaghilev's main interest but with the introduction of theatrical performances he was able to call in his friends from the old group. Encouraged especially by Benois and Bakst he included in the 1909 Russian season in Paris the operas *Ivan the Terrible* and *Russlan and Ludmila*, the dances from *Prince Igor* by Alexander Borodin and a number of short ballets such as *Le Pavillon d'Armide*, *Cléopâtre*, *Les Sylphides* and *Le Festin*.

Above
Fyodor Chaliapine as Boris in Boris Godunov *by Modest Mussorgsky, St Petersburg 1905. The opera was first performed at the Imperial Opera in St Petersburg in 1874*

Right
Costume design for Boris Godunov. *The Tsarevitch in prison. Painted in 1908 by Ivan Bilibin*

The Parisians were impressed by the splendour of the opera productions, but were quite overwhelmed by the ballets, which were far in advance of anything produced elsewhere in Europe in terms of their choreography, music and design. French ballet was still resting on the laurels of the 1840s, although there was a more recent and degenerate music-hall element with male roles being taken by women *en travestie*.

From 1910 Diaghilev concentrated on the ballet and his company became known as Les Ballets Russes. The great triumph of the 1910 season was *Schéhérazade*, a ballet that still shocks and overwhelms with Bakst's seething set and Fokine's intensely erotic choreography. Musically, the most important event was the production of Stravinksy's first ballet, *The Firebird*, but the repertoire also included *Giselle* and *Carnaval*. The season was an overwhelming success and left the French public panting for more.

Although he might have been tempted to extend the season if he had been able, Diaghilev did not have a permanent company; his dancers returned to jobs in Russia after the temporary excitements of the Paris season. On his next visit to St Petersburg, however, Diaghilev was party to a silly incident that was responsible for a dramatic change in his position.

The one dancer whose presence was absolutely essential to the success of any season planned by Diaghilev was, of course, Vaslav Nijinsky. Nijinsky was under strict contractual obligations to the Imperial Ballet. Nevertheless, as the result of a scene no doubt partly orchestrated by Diaghilev, Nijinsky was able to dispense with his official ties. A performance of *Giselle* was announced with Nijinsky in the principal male role of Albrecht. Nijinsky insisted on wearing the first act costume that Benois had designed for the production of the ballet in Paris. The costume, with no trunks and a short tunic, was much more scanty than the costume traditionally used at the Imperial Ballet, and was thought rather shocking. Nijinsky was asked to revert to the costume he had worn previously in St Petersburg but he refused and was promptly suspended by the directorate of the Imperial Ballet. Neither side would back down and Nijinsky was dismissed from the Imperial Ballet and free to become the star of Diaghilev's company.

Other dancers followed him so that by 1911 the Ballets Russes developed from a rather casual grouping of Russian

Scene from Schéhérazade, *painted in about 1910 by Lucien Lelong*

dancers taking time off from their real work at the Imperial Ballet into a permanent company. The base for its activities was, of course, Paris but Diaghilev never managed to find a permanent theatre there and it led a nomadic existence. In 1911 the company performed in London, Rome and Monte Carlo as well as in Paris and from 1912 the wanderings became truly international.

The creation of the Ballets Russes reached its climax in 1911, the year of *Petrushka*. The season also included *Narcisse*, *Le Spectre de la Rose*, and *Sadko*, as well as revivals from the two previous seasons, but it was *Petrushka* that best expressed the personality of the company. Audiences flocked to see the great dancers of the Ballets Russes such as Nijinsky and Karsavina. Initially attracted by the excitement of the big name or the whiff of scandal, they were quick to appreciate the colour, spectacle and sheer exoticism of a ballet such as *Petrushka*.

The next three years saw a consolidation of the position of the Ballets Russes, both with extended seasons in Paris and tours to many parts of Europe. Fokine's *Daphnis and Chloe* was the most important ballet of the 1912 season although Nijinsky's dancing and choreography for *L'Après-midi d'un Faune* perhaps attracted more attention. Nijinsky also choreographed *Jeux* and *Le Sacre du Printemps*, the two most celebrated ballets produced for the 1913 season. Nijinsky's marriage and subsequent break with Diaghilev at the end of 1913 really marked the end of the first heady period of the Ballets Russes. Fokine returned as choreographer in 1914, and Benois reappeared, advising in the wings, but the initial whirl of romantic-cum-revolutionary glamour was gone. Diaghilev visited the United States in 1916 and spent the next eight years desperately trying to assure the future of his famous but economically precarious creation, not aided by his new production of *The Sleeping Princess* in 1921, a major financial disaster.

Finally, in 1923, Diaghilev found a home for his company in the monied artistic enclave of Monte Carlo. He continued to employ new composers, choreographers, (notably Bronislava Nijinska) and artists, presenting a glittering array of ballets, not only new and exciting works but also lavish revivals. The tremendous reputation of the Ballets Russes, however, relied on the memory of the first triumphant seasons in Paris when works like *Petrushka* had persuaded the West that ballet really was a higher form of art.

Vaslav Nijinsky (1889–1950) in L'Après-midi d'un Faune, *painted in about 1912 by Dorothy Muller. The ballet with designs by Leon Bakst was one of three choreographed by Nijinsky*

The Creation of Petrushka

The origins of *Petrushka*, along with many of Diaghilev's ballets, are still confused. In the afterglow of success generated by the ballet, both Stravinsky and Benois bubbled over with mutual affection, each trying to credit the other with the lion's share of the ballet's creation. The idea began with Stravinsky who, encouraged by Diaghilev, went to Benois to have his thoughts organized and developed. Most writers, Benois himself prominent among them, have given the libretto, almost in its entirety, to Benois, but more recently Stravinsky has been considered responsible for the ballet—both libretto and music. However, Benois' contribution must have been fundamental, even allowing for some embroidery in his memoirs; he was experienced in the art of crafting ballet libretti; the subject was one especially close to his heart and his literary mind was able to organize and control Stravinsky's musical creativity as well as his original conception.

Unfortunately, Benois was not available to write the libretto in 1910, when Stravinsky first presented Diaghilev with the idea of a ballet about a puppet. He had left the Ballets Russes in high dudgeon after his libretto for *Schéhérazade* had been attributed to Bakst in the programmes of the 1910 Paris performances.

It is possible that Diaghilev had provoked the quarrel deliberately, thinking that he could dispense with the services of his old friend; Stravinsky, after all, was supposed to be working on the score of a ballet based on a primitive pagan rite (not a subject that would appeal to Benois) which became *Le Sacre du Printemps* in 1913. According to Benois, Diaghilev and Nijinsky had visited him in Lugano to try to persuade him to return to the Ballets Russes after the row over *Schéhérazade*. He was convalescing in Switzerland after smashing a window with his fist in his anger at Diaghilev's behaviour. Benois refused, but changed his mind once back in St Petersburg when he heard from Diaghilev about Stravinsky's ballet *Petrushka*.

At this point, Stravinsky had written two pieces for the ballet, a Russian Dance and the piece he called 'Petrushka's Cry'. Diaghilev saw immediately how useful Benois could be, knowing that puppets, side-shows, and street entertainments were his especial love, and contacted him in St Petersburg straight away. Petrushka, the Russian equivalent of Punch in *Punch and Judy*, was a great favourite with children. From his earliest years Benois had followed the puppet's violent and ultimately fatal career in the puppet booths erected in the courtyard of his own house, as well as during the annual Butter Week Fair in St

Above
Petrushka and the Ballerina, painted in 1945 by Alexandre Benois

Right
Igor Stravinsky (1882–1971) by Jean Cocteau
Second right
Alexandre Benois (1870–1960), pastel drawing by Constantin Somov

Petersburg. Diaghilev suggested that the ballet should be set during this Fair, held in the week before Lent, at a date around 1830, a period close to Benois' heart.

Out of this interesting but possibly unpromising material was fashioned one of the most intensely moving ballets ever

Above
Caricature of Serge Diaghilev by Jean Cocteau

created. Petrushka himself was quickly changed from a marionette with legs dangling uselessly over the edge of the stage, his usual form in the street booths, to a full-length puppet. He was also given two companions, a stupid but pretty ballerina and a virile blackamoor. The street perform-ances of *Petrushka* invariably included an intermezzo in which two smartly dressed blackamoors set about each other with excessive violence and long sticks. Benois toyed with the stick before turning the moor's props into a sabre and a coconut. The three dolls were to be controlled by a magician who had given his creation almost perfect human souls as well as almost perfect human bodies.

The libretto had reached this stage when Stravinsky visited St Petersburg to discuss the progress of the ballet with Benois. The two men must have come to a fairly close understanding of how the work would develop as Stravin-sky returned quickly to Switzerland and it was six months before they saw each other again. Their discussions seem to have centred on the creation of the two big Fair scenes, the first scene and the last. Stravinsky introduced organ-

grinders and drunken men with accordions, Benois suggested various folk songs as well as gypsies and mummers,
and in a letter Diaghilev added his own suggestions of
grooms and coachmen beating their hands to keep warm.
The suggestions were incorporated into the libretto and
music as the letters whizzed between Switzerland, Paris
and St Petersburg.

While composing the libretto, Benois was also designing
the costumes and no doubt sent versions of these to
Stravinsky to express his ideas for the ballet in as graphic a
way as possible. The three men met again in Rome in the
spring of 1911. The Ballets Russes were performing at the
Teatro Costanza during a World Exhibition, and the first
rehearsals of Petrushka took place in the basement buffet of
the theatre. The music and libretto were finished some time
after rehearsals began, the second scene with Petrushka's
death being the last part to be completed. At this point
Fokine took over, endlessly rehearsing his three soloists,
Nijinsky, Karsavina, and Orlov and, when possible, his
crowd of extras, gradually giving concrete form to the work.

Keith Rosson, Jennifer
Penney and Alexander
Grant as the Moor, the
Ballerina and Petrushka.
Royal Ballet, 1966

The Music

Igor Stravinsky painted in 1915 by Jacques-Emile Blanche. During the First World War, lacking the large resources which had previously been available to him, Stravinsky concentrated on works for the theatre such as Renard *and* The Soldier's Tale

Igor Stravinsky was born in 1882 in St Petersburg. The son of a singer at the Imperial Russian Opera, he studied under Rimsky-Korsakov and was much influenced by his teaching. When Diaghilev commissioned him to write the music for *The Firebird* in 1909 he accidentally discovered the major source of music for twentieth-century ballet. Stravinsky eventually composed twenty works for the stage including sixteen ballets and over a hundred of his other compositions have been used subsequently by many choreographers for their ballets. His first three ballet scores, *The*

Firebird, *Petrushka* and *Le Sacre du Printemps*, were arguably the three works which secured the reputation of the Ballets Russes.

It was hoped initially that Tcherepnin would write the score for *The Firebird*, the ballet conceived mainly by Fokine but also by others of Diaghilev's circle in order to satisfy the Parisian demand for a work with a Russian theme. However, Tcherepnin lost interest and Lyadov was offered the job. It was assumed that Lyadov was working hard at the score until it was discovered, rather late in the

Marguerite Porter in the title-role of The Firebird, *Royal Ballet, 1982. The costumes and scenery are by Natalia Gontcharova who redesigned the ballet for the revival by Diaghilev in 1926*

day, that he had only just bought his manuscript music paper and had not written a note. Diaghilev quickly passed the commission on to Stravinsky, a young composer whose career had hardly begun but whose *Fantastic Scherzo* and *Fireworks* Diaghilev had recently heard at a St Petersburg concert. The work, intended for 1909, was postponed for a year and Stravinsky was soon working in close liaison with Fokine, who was to choreograph the ballet. This partnership produced a ballet in which the choreographic and musical images related one to the other in an unprecedented way. The episodic inevitability of the classical ballet was replaced by a much more exciting and original dance in which Fokine created a free and natural form of movement which reflected the unexpected rhythms and repeated motifs of the music. The unique balance of the ballet was enhanced by the designs, by Golovine and Bakst, which were strongly influenced by Fokine's desire for an overall concept dictated by the music but expressed both in the movement and in the scenery and costumes.

The production of *The Firebird*, which opened at the Paris Opéra on 25 June 1910, was a great success and encouraged Diaghilev to commission more work from Stravinsky. He was inspired with ideas for a new ballet which were to result in *Le Sacre du Printemps*, eventually finished three years later. Tiring slightly of the ballet, however, he began to work on a concert piece which he planned to be 'a kind of combat between piano and orchestra'. He went to Switzerland with his family and began to write: 'Before getting down to *Le Sacre du Printemps*, which I knew would be a long and laborious task, I wanted to amuse myself with an orchestral piece in which the piano would play the principal part, a sort of *Konzertstück*. In composing this music I had a clear vision of a puppet, suddenly brought to life, and who also tries the patience of the orchestra with cascades of diabolical arpeggios. The orchestra, in turn, replies with menacing fanfares. Finally, there is a terrible din which, reaching a climax, ends in the sad and plaintive collapse of the poor puppet.'

Stravinsky could not think of a title for the piece but by the time Diaghilev and Nijinsky came to visit him in September 1910 he had decided on *Petrushka*, the traditional Russian puppet. Whether or not Stravinsky intended to use his score as a ballet does not seem to have worried Diaghilev. He immediately saw the potential of the piece as a work for the Ballets Russes and wrote to Benois in St Petersburg.

Page from the score of Petrushka, 1911, *with numerous annotations by Stravinsky*

Meanwhile Stravinsky concentrated on the development of the music. The clash of puppet and orchestra resolved itself musically into the clash of two major triads, C and F sharp, or white notes versus black notes. This became Petrushka's fanfare motif which is heard throughout the ballet; it appears to greatest effect right at the end of the piece to show that Petrushka's ghost is still there, mocking and insulting the foolish crowd. Although Fokine thought that this musical concept was too simplistic for the complicated crowd scenes, the bitonality does help to create a feeling of bustle and of different things happening at the same time. Bearing in mind the Parisian desire for artistic expressions of Russian nationalism, Stravinsky managed to weave into his music any number of popular Russian folk songs. He also included themes from less original or ethnic sources, such as the Josef Lanner waltz which is used to accompany a *pas de deux* for the Ballerina and the Moor. Unfortunately, Stravinsky went too far in his enthusiasm for popular melodies and found himself having to pay royalties (until the 1950s) to the writer of a popular song, 'Elle avait une jambe en bois', which somehow found its way into the score.

Stravinsky revised and arranged the music a number of times. It was first heard in a concert performance in Paris in 1914 and the original time of forty-two or three minutes was cut down to a suite lasting about twenty. This, according to Stravinsky, consisted of 'the Hocus-Pocus, the Russian Dance, the entire second scene, and the fourth scene ending in a specially orchestrated trill by the full orchestra on F-sharp . . .' In 1919, Stravinsky permitted the Aeolian Company of London to transcribe both *Petrushka* and *Le Sacre du Printemps* onto piano rolls and himself provided Artur Rubinstein with a virtuoso transcription for piano in 1921. After failing to persuade Benois to agree to a sound film of *Petrushka* in 1929, Stravinsky received $10,000 in 1956 when he conducted fifteen minutes of the music as a sound track for an animated cartoon film.

Petrushka was an advance in every way on *The Firebird*, choreographically, scenically and, especially, musically. The brilliance and inventiveness of *The Firebird* were complemented by a wealth of new expressiveness as well as concise detail. With *Petrushka*, Stravinsky was recognized as a major composer, a position he consolidated with the score of *Le Sacre du Printemps*, a scandal and disaster when first performed, but acknowledged today as a masterpiece.

The Designs

Both Benois and Stravinsky had vivid childhood memories of street performances of *Petrushka* but Benois, much the more articulate of the two men, was able to describe the performances in his extensive memoirs. He also recalled the great Butter Week Fairs of his childhood, the setting he created for the ballet. Benois remembered one of the last Butter Week Fairs in the centre of St Petersburg. The venue had already changed from Admiralty Square, where *Petrushka* takes place, to Winter Palace Square and in 1875 it moved again, to the Tsar's Meadow or the Champ de Mars. Benois' strongest memory was of the Finnish sleighs which drove about the streets of St Petersburg during the week of the Fair, arriving on the Sunday before Lent.

The square was occupied by large numbers of temporary buildings, on one side the pinewood theatres, large and imposing, and on the other side the less impressive side-shows, as well as the booths selling sweets, biscuits and toys. There were also roundabouts, erected inside a large hut because of the intense cold. The walls of the hut were painted in a rather haphazard way with landscapes, comic genre scenes and portraits of famous generals and beautiful ladies. From a balcony, the *Dyed* or 'Grandfather' would call to all and sundry, sometimes while standing on his head, and invite them in. He was accompanied by two skippety dancers and two peculiar beasts, a goat and a crane, who appeared only from time to time. There were also peep-shows with the showman adding a commentary to the necessarily short visual experience. A travelling zoo was full of mangy animals but its hut was brightly painted with a tropical forest of palm trees and exotic flowers. Benois recalled being unimpressed by the animals but quite overwhelmed by the resident ballerina who wore a spangled skirt and a thick black beard.

At least one of the large theatres showed harlequinades and if Benois' description is accurate they must have achieved a high level of technical sophistication, with many transformation scenes and quick-change artistes jumping through innumerable trap-doors. From 1880 the harlequinades were replaced by Russian folk dramas, melodramatic and intensely moralistic. The Fairs were always remarkable for the quantity of liquor consumed and after they were banished to the suburbs the Fairs died a slow and sober death, brought about largely by Prince Oldenburg and the Temperance Society.

The setting of the Butter Week Fair in Admiralty Square was used in all the productions of *Petrushka* designed by Benois—he designed at least eleven – all based on the

Design for a carnival costume for the 1957 Royal Ballet production of Petrushka *by Alexandre Benois after an original design of 1911*

original 1911 production. A feature that remained common to all Benois productions was the false proscenium which gave an extra dimension to the idea of watching a play within a play, confusing the boundaries between performance and reality. Benois' frame was always in a deliberately 'folksy' Russian style, painted bright cobalt blue and decorated with square window frames whose shutters were painted with gaily coloured flower-pots. The naïvety of the frame contrasted with the looped crimson curtain hanging behind, which revealed a sophisticated view of St Petersburg with the tall cupola of St Isaac's Cathedral towering above the teeming life of the carnival below. Benois seems to have been anxious to reproduce the topography of the area as accurately as possible, although his sketches of the architectural detail of the cathedral show that he had some difficulty in working out the correct perspective for the scene.

The first scene, with the Fair in the foreground, had a similar grandiose architectural background. The scene takes place, of course, in Admiralty Square, and everything is dominated by the classical spire of the Admiralty. This large scene, with its crowds, stalls and booths, occupied most of Benois' energy and time on *Petrushka*. The costumes were all from Benois' favourite period of the 1830s and whilst the drawings, of samovars for instance, show an unerring feel and concern for accurate detail, there is always a sympathetic sense of humour in the costume designs. Other designs, such as those for the frieze of paintings over the showman's booth, reflect Benois' encyclopedic knowledge of Russian folk art.

The curtain lowered between the scenes originally showed the evil Showman holding a flute and surrounded by clouds. In later productions this was replaced by a vivid dark blue night sky with huge monstrous spirits skidding across it.

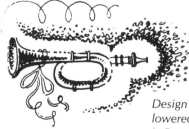

Design for the drop curtain lowered between the scenes in Petrushka *for the 1952 La Scala, Milan production in 1952 by Alexandre Benois*

Petrushka's cubicle, the second scene, was dominated by the portrait of the evil Showman. This was damaged in transit from St Petersburg to Paris, and Bakst's 'repair', in which the profile portrait was replaced by a full-face portrait, caused a great rift between Benois and Diaghilev. Benois' original idea was reinstated, but the row marked the end of Benois' connection with the Ballets Russes for some time.

The third scene, showing the Moor's room, seems to have given Benois considerable trouble. He was uncertain just how exotic to make the wall-covering and he settled on his final design of huge exotic trees and flowers only after experimenting with menageries of elephants, lions, crocodiles and the rest of the African jungle, a frieze of extraordinary trees turning into even more extraordinary dream-like monsters and various friezes of palm trees, some more and some a great deal less than realistic. The general feeling of zany exoticism always remained the same, however, and contrasted strongly with the sombre loneliness of Petrushka's cubicle.

The final scene is a return to the bustle of the first, although Benois originally had the idea of an interlude showing the Admiralty Square, deserted and by moonlight. Benois' designs for *Petrushka* grew and developed as the ballet itself was being created and have almost always been an integral part of subsequent interpretations.

Right
Design for Petrushka's room for the 1952 production at La Scala, Milan by Alexandre Benois, based on his original design of 1911

Left
Design for a pancake-seller for the 1957 Royal Ballet production by Alexandre Benois

Right
Design for the Moor's room for the 1952 La Scala, Milan production, a variant of his original design by Alexandre Benois

The Choreography

Mikhail Fokine was undoubtedly one of the most important and original choreographers of the twentieth century, and *Petrushka* was possibly his most original work. Born into a middle-class family in St Petersburg in 1880, Fokine was accepted by the Imperial Ballet School at the age of nine, much against his father's will. He graduated in 1898 and made his début at the Maryinsky Theatre in the same year. Although he became one of the major young dancers of the Imperial Ballet, he was not satisfied with merely being a dancer; he was far too curious, inventive and creative to be just another interpreter of other people's work. He started to teach at the Imperial School in 1902; first small girls, then the older girls and then, in about 1905, he began to teach the boys as well. Although he encountered a certain amount of opposition at the ballet school, he was given the opportunity to create new ballets for student performances.

Illustration to Daphnis and Chloe, *painted in 1914 by George Barbier*

It was an opportunity he took extremely seriously, seeing the chance to break out of the overbearing and fusty traditions of the Imperial Ballet. He believed strongly in the need for a perfect classical technique which he had gained from the school and which, in any case, he continued to teach, but he challenged the predictable nature of certain aspects of Russian ballet in performance. For instance, he doubted that a pirouette or a double turn in the air was an absolutely indispensable finish to each male dancer's variation, although the Imperial Ballet dancers seemed to think otherwise. He also disagreed with the convention that the body should always be straight and facing the audience and that the arms should be held in a stereotyped circle. He was annoyed by the custom of the dancers milking applause for each acrobatic feat and estimated that a variation lasting forty-eight bars was invariably matched by forty-eight bars of applause.

His new approach to choreography was, of course, a reflection of his method of teaching which he describes in his autobiography: 'I tried to give a meaning to the movements and poses; I tried not to make the dance resemble gymnastics. I endeavoured to make the student aware of the music so he would not treat it as a mere accompaniment. I tried to make the student not content with having just a superficial connection between the movement or a measure of the music, or part of a measure, but seek to interpret the phrases, the accents, the musical nuances and whole phrases. I stressed the extension of the lines of the body.'

In his first ballet for the Imperial Ballet School, *Acis and Galatea*, which was performed in 1905, Fokine tried to introduce the new ideas expressed in the libretto of *Daphnis and Chloe*, submitted to the Director of the Imperial Ballet, Teliakovsky, the previous year. Fokine suggested that 'The ballet should be staged in conformity with the epoch represented; that the dance pantomimes and gestures should not be of the conventional style established in the old ballet but should be of a kind that best fits the style of the period. The costumes also should not be of the established ballet style but be consistent with the plot; that the ballet must be uninterrupted—a complete artistic creation and not a series of separate numbers; that in the interests of retaining scenic illusion the action must not be interrupted with applause and its acknowledgment by the artists; that the music should not consist of waltzes, polkas, and final galops, but must express the story of the ballet and, primarily, its emotional content.'

Mikhail Fokine as Daphnis and Vera Fokina as Chloe in Daphnis and Chloe, *Ballets Russes, Monte Carlo 1914*

In the event, *Acis and Galatea* was something of a compromise, but Fokine was satisfied that his ideas were beginning to make an impact. In *Eunice* of 1907, another ballet dealing with a classical theme, Fokine believed that the conception and style of the ancient dance which he had introduced were finally accepted: 'I entirely excluded the turnout of the feet, the dances on *pointe*, and such typical ballet steps as the *pirouette*, *entrechat*, *rond de jambes*, as well as various *battements* and the like. But besides the technical differences between my Greek dances and those of the old ballets, I was able to achieve a very plastic approach which has come down to us from the ancient world. *Arabesques*, *attitudes*, straightening-out of polelike legs in the fourth position, and the rounded (*en couronne*) arms over the head—all this was omitted whenever a ballet of mine dealt with themes on ancient subjects.' In the same year as *Eunice* Fokine created *Chopiniana*, which later became *Les Sylphides*, showing that he was as happy working in the Romantic tradition as he was with his new, revolutionary methods. In fact, he was violently opposed to altering the work of other, more traditional choreographers, always preferring to work with new material.

Perhaps the most important new material Fokine was able to use in 1907 was Tcherepnin's score for *Le Pavillon d'Armide* because work on this ballet led Fokine directly to his collaboration with Benois and Diaghilev. The ballet was created originally using a suite from a larger score, as a graduation exercise for Imperial Ballet students. The work impressed the Imperial Ballet Theatre directors and the full-length *Pavillon d'Armide* was produced eventually at the Maryinsky Theatre. Benois not only wrote the libretto but also created the costumes and scenery, and Fokine thrilled to his whimsical Louis xiv designs. However, the two men disagreed violently over the nature of the ballet, Fokine preferring a much curtailed version to Benois' old-fashioned liking for interminable repetition. Benois, however, also assisted Fokine with his next ballet, *Nuits Égyptiennes*, although when it was shown as *Cléopâtre* in Paris, the designs were by Bakst. And it was Benois who informed Fokine of the proposed Russian ballet season in Paris in 1909 and introduced him to Diaghilev. As a result of the introduction Fokine staged the Polovtsian Dances

Design for the second tableau in Le Pavillon d'Armide, *painted in 1953 after his original design of 1909 by Alexandre Benois*

from *Prince Igor*, *Les Sylphides* and *Cléopâtre* during the first season and returned to Paris in 1910 to stage *Schéhérazade* and *The Firebird*.

These two ballets were of fundamental importance to the later production of *Petrushka*. In *The Firebird* Fokine collaborated with Stravinsky for the first time and in *Schéhérazade* he began to apply his new theories. Actions and emotions were expressed through movements and positions of the body rather than with the traditional speaking gestures of the hands. As Fokine said, '*Schéhérazade* contained love and passion, guilt, treachery, and anger, grief and desperation, and there were no hand gesticulations'.

The production of *The Firebird* arose from Diaghilev's desire to give the Parisians a 'ballet of Russian life' for his 1910 season. In fact, the Parisians themselves, excited by the Polovtsian Dances were anxious to see more ethnic expression. Stravinsky and Fokine worked very closely together on *The Firebird*, both music and choreography being created simultaneously. Fokine was never able to repeat the experience of such a close collaboration with either Stravinsky or any other composer and when asked to stage *Petrushka* in 1911, he was presented with a complete, or nearly complete, score and libretto.

Fokine first heard the score to *Petrushka* played by an unenthusiastic pianist who had no feeling at all for the music. Even so the images of Petrushka and the Blackamoor evidently made a considerable impression and he was able to form a more concrete picture when Stravinsky himself played it to him. Although Fokine had some reservations about the music, he approached it with his usual professionalism. He was a good musician, playing several instruments, and had orchestrated a number of works for an amateur orchestra with which he used to play.

Fokine's command of the music was a great help when working with dancers such as Nijinsky who did not, perhaps, have such a strong musical sense. All the dancers memorized by ear, and Fokine frequently needed to explain the complex beat and rhythm. The most difficult part for the ensemble in *Petrushka* is the finale, and the rapid 5/8 beat caused so much confusion for the dancers in rehearsal that Fokine had to gather everyone around the

Petrushka falls dead from a blow delivered by the Moor's scimitar while the stunned crowd looks on. Photograph from a Diaghilev album, Ballets Russes, Paris 1911

piano for clapping sessions, an exercise that had to be repeated many times.

The crowd scenes in *Petrushka*, with over a hundred people on stage, were extremely difficult to organize; some developed spontaneously in rehearsal and were adopted by Fokine. Stravinsky complained that the ensemble was somewhat sloppy but Fokine blamed the music saying that Stravinsky had provided only two themes for the great variety of characters. Each dancer, however, was given a role and each one was supposed to remain strictly in character. The crowd had to be as vigorous and as alive as possible in order to make the three puppets seem more doll-like. Of the three dolls, the Ballerina was the most mechanical in her movements. Hoping, in her tutu, to avoid what Fokine once called 'the stereotyped and dreary image of the ballerina', she had to be both extremely pretty and extremely silly. Karsavina played the part entirely to Fokine's satisfaction, allowing herself not a whisper of improvisation. Fokine spent a great deal of time rehearsing her, cutting down her movements to the bare expressive essentials. The other two dolls, the Moor and Petrushka himself, were given simple but fundamental choreographic personalities; the Moor was all *en dehors* (turned out) to represent his expansive, extroverted personality, and Petrushka was all *en dedans* (turned in) to express his painful introverted personality. All the choreography for these two characters was based on this fundamental concept and the main conflict of the drama simply and clearly depicted.

Diaghilev recognized the choreographic integrity of *Petrushka* after the triumph of the Paris première, and knew perfectly well the value of Fokine as his resident choreographer. By the 1912 season, however, his infatuation with Nijinsky had reached such epic proportions that he was prepared to dispense with Fokine's services as choreographer in favour of Nijinsky. Nijinsky's *L'Après-midi d'un Faune* took precedence over Fokine's much more important *Daphnis et Chloe*, and the association of choreographer and impresario crumbled. Fokine returned in 1914 to stage *Le Coq d'Or* and *La Legende de Joseph* but the renewed contact did not last and Fokine spent most of his later years tilling the, as yet, barren soil of American ballet.

Tamara Karsavina as the Ballerina, Paris 1911. Her pose is far from that of the conventional ballerina. In Petrushka Fokine's ideals of expressive choreography have their most successful representation. The ballet's great achievement is the fusion of the two elements of mime and choreography so that the whole ballet relates to the spirit of the libretto

Nijinsky as Petrushka

I should like at this point to pay heartfelt homage to Vaslav Nijinsky's unsurpassed rendering of the role of Petrouschka. The perfection with which he became the very incarnation of this character was all the more remarkable because of the purely saltatory work in which he usually excelled was in this case definitely dominated by dramatic action, music and gestures.

Stravinsky's curiously worded praise of Nijinsky reflected the dancer's ability to lose himself entirely in the role he was playing. When he played Petrushka the audience was quite unaware of his extraordinary physique, his Slavic features, his virtuoso technique and his classical discipline. Instead they saw a dusty doll with wooden limbs, his baked face punctured with currant-like eyes, painfully executing a series of peculiar jerking movements which somehow added up to one of the most moving depictions of character ever seen in a ballet.

Benois noted that Nijinsky had been unable to understand his part during rehearsals and had even asked him to explain the role. On the night, however, Nijinsky's astounding grasp of character did not fail him and Benois noted the transformation: 'The metamorphosis took place when he put on his costume and covered his face with make-up—I was surprised at the courage Vaslav showed, after all his *jeune premier* successes, in appearing as a horrible half-doll, half-human grotesque. The great difficulty of Petroushka's part is to express his pitiful oppression and his hopeless efforts to achieve personal dignity without ceasing to be a puppet. Both music and libretto are spasmodically interrupted by outbursts of illusive joy and frenzied despair. The artist is not given a single *pas* or *fioriture* to enable him to be attractive to the public, and one must remember that Nijinsky was then quite a young man and the temptation to "be attractive to the public" must have appealed to him far more strongly than to an older artist.'

Nijinsky was unique in the entire history of dance in his ability to recreate himself in the mould of the character he was performing. Even so, the part of Petrushka was perhaps a special case and it is probably true to say that as Petrushka, Nijinsky was typecast. The parallel between the Showman and Petrushka on the one hand and Diaghilev and Nijinsky on the other may seem facile but it is certainly one that many contemporaries found convincing. Benois, in particular, indicated as much in one of his drawings, showing Nijinsky under the shadow of Diaghilev.

Above and right
Vaslav Nijinsky as Petrushka, Paris 1911. Nijinsky was the first dancer who worked closely with photographers to reveal the artistry both in ballet and in his own performance

Petrushka since 1911

There have been at least eighty revivals of *Petrushka* since 1911. The most extraordinary thing about them is not the great number of productions but the fact that the vast majority have used Benois' original designs and many have reproduced Fokine's original choreography. There is evidently a general and tacit belief in *Petrushka* as the perfect ballet. Of course, there have been a number of exceptions—the time-hallowed integrity of *Petrushka* being a sufficient temptation for change to some designers and choreographers.

Choreographers such as John Neumeier, at the Schwetzingen Festival in 1976, and Maurice Béjart, in Brussels in 1977, evidently felt it necessary to produce new versions of the ballet to excite a complacent public out of its cultural lethargy. In Béjart's version the action is brought forward to the present day and the two underlying themes of Petrushka's crisis of identity and the problems of the eternal triangle are explored in a more explicit way than in the original libretto. For Béjart, Petrushka becomes merely 'a young man', the Ballerina is his girlfriend, 'a young girl' and the Moor becomes another young man, 'the friend'.

The ballet begins with the three young people enjoying a visit to a fair when a Magician suddenly appears and conjures up a strange castle, magical and surreal. He then proceeds to dance with three masks which depict Petrushka, the Ballerina and the Moor. His friends find the performance amusing but the young man is profoundly disturbed and charges into the Magician's castle. Once inside he finds a labyrinth of mirrors and the three masks. He tries on the Petrushka mask and takes it off. He finds, however, that his features remain those of Petrushka and the image multiplies in the mirrors to taunt and chase him. He goes through the same process with the other two masks and relives the story of the puppets. The young man becomes so distressed that when the Magician reappears he seems to lose control of himself and dances wildly, in great agitation.

Meanwhile, the fair continues and when the young man leaves the Magician's castle, initially dazed but gradually regaining his wits, he finds that his girl friend still loves him and that his friend is genuinely affectionate. At a signal from the Magician, however doubts set in and the young man sees everything turned upside-down; his fiancée is being unfaithful with the friend; he sees masks mocking him everywhere he turns and he loses all sense of judgement, reason and personality. The Magician calls and he follows him into the magical labyrinth.

Richard Cragun as Petrushka in the Stuttgart Ballet version of Maurice Béjart's production

Although Béjart has kept the theme of *Petrushka* in the most general of terms and the original setting of a fair, it was only Stravinsky's music that he regarded as sacrosanct. The idea of a fundamental change to the ballet libretto with the retention of the music was not new and had been at least suggested a quarter of a century before Béjart's production was mounted.

In a letter of 23 August 1950, Lincoln Kirstein wrote to Stravinsky discussing a proposed season of Stravinsky ballets to be given in London by the New York City Ballet. He suggested that the season would be 'vindictive and triumphal' and would include, 'what will kill them, lacking Nijinsky, Benois and Fokine—the new *Petrushka*. . .' The production was to have been designed by Pavel Tchelitchev who saw the ballet in exclusively universal terms, 'subject to universal symbolic laws', and originating, like all fairy-tales, in the 'magico-religious'. He saw the ballet as a conflict between the body (the Moor), the soul or anima (the Ballerina) and the spirit (Petrushka). Stravinsky found Tchelitchev's theories somewhat daunting and preferred the more down to earth and passive interpretation he expected to get from Chagall. In the event, the production was abandoned.

Despite the success of Vladimir Vassiliev as the young man in Béjart's 1977 production of *Petrushka*, the greatest

Below
Peter Clegg as the Moor, Margot Fonteyn as the Ballerina and Alexander Grant as Petrushka. Royal Ballet, 1957

interpreters of the principal role in the ballet, such as Mikhail Baryshnikov with American Ballet Theatre, have relied largely on the inspiration they found in keeping close to the original choreography. A faithful reconstruction of Fokine's choreography was used by the Royal Ballet in 1957 in its first production of the ballet with Alexander Grant as Petrushka, Peter Clegg as the Moor, and Margot Fonteyn the Ballerina. Nadia Nerina also played the Ballerina in some performances and subsequent Petrushkas included Brian Shaw and Rudolf Nureyev. Peter Schaufuss took the role in London Festival Ballet in 1971, Nureyev was the first Petrushka in the John Taras production for the Royal Ballet in 1975, and John Bintley was· perhaps the most distinctive of the three alternative Petrushkas in John Auld's 1984 production for Sadler's Wells Royal Ballet. In *Petrushka* Fokine combined the elements of mime and choreography in such a way that the two are indistinguishable. It was the culmination of his work as a choreographer and is the first major step in the history of twentieth-century ballet.

Above
David Bintley as Petrushka.
Sadler's Wells Royal Ballet,
1984

Rudolf Nureyev as the dying
Petrushka in the last scene.
Royal Ballet, 1975

48

Index

Acknowledgments
Bibliothèque Nationale 24–5;
Bibliothèque de l'Opéra, Paris 19, 34, 39, 40, 41;
Mike Davis 2–3;
Dominic Photography 44, 45–7;
E T Archive 32;
Marina Henderson Gallery, London 17, 27, 29, 30, 31, 34–5;
Nikita Lobanov 9, 11;
Novosti Press Agency 12;
Private Collection 14–5, 19;
Réunion des Musées Nationaux 22;
Sothebys 6–7, 13, 19;
Leslie Spatt 43, 45;
Victoria and Albert Museum 1, 36–7;
Reg Wilson 20–1, 23